JUNE 50 COLORING PAGES FOR ADULTS RELAXATION

SHIH CHIEN HUA

PUBLISHED BY:
SHIH CHIEN HUA
Copyright © 2018

SEABIRD SHOP >50FOR

FB FAN PAGE

Disclaimer
The information contained in this book is for general information purposes only. The information is provided by the authors and while we endeavor to keep the information up to date and correct, we make no representations or warranties of any kind, express or implied, about the completeness, accuracy, reliability, suitability or availability with respect to the book or the information, products, services, or related graphics contained in the book for any purpose. Any reliance you place on such information is therefore strictly at your own risk.

JUNE 1ST

note:

_____

_____

_____

JUNE 2ND

note:

_____

_____

_____

JUNE 3RD

note:

_____

_____

_____

JUNE 4TH

note:

_____

_____

_____

JUNE 5TH

note:

_____

_____

_____

JUNE 6TH

note:

_____

_____

_____

JUNE 7TH

note:

_____

_____

_____

JUNE 8TH

note:

_____

_____

_____

JUNE 9TH

note:

_____

_____

_____

JUNE 10TH

note:

_____

_____

_____

JUNE 11TH

note:

_____

_____

_____

JUNE 12TH

note:

_____

_____

_____

JUNE 13TH

note:

_____

_____

_____

JUNE 14TH

note:

_____

_____

_____

JUNE 15TH

note:

_____

_____

_____

JUNE 16TH

note:

_____

_____

_____

JUNE 17TH

note:

_____

_____

_____

JUNE 18TH

note:

_____

_____

_____

JUNE 19TH

note:

_____

_____

_____

JUNE 20TH

note:

_____

_____

_____

JUNE 21TH

note:

_____

_____

_____

JUNE 22TH

note:

_____

_____

_____

JUNE 23TH

note:

_____

_____

_____

JUNE 24TH

note:

_____

_____

_____

JUNE 25TH

note:

_____

_____

_____

JUNE 26TH

note:

_____

_____

_____

JUNE 27TH

note:

_____

_____

_____

JUNE 28TH

note:

_____

_____

_____

JUNE 29TH

note:

_____

_____

_____

JUNE 30TH

note:

_____

_____

_____

JUNE 31TH

note:

_____

_____

_____

JUNE 32TH

note:

_____

_____

_____

JUNE 33TH

note:

_____

_____

_____

JUNE 34TH

note:

_____

_____

_____

JUNE 35TH

note:

_____

_____

_____

JUNE 36TH

note:

_____

_____

_____

JUNE 37TH

note:

_____

_____

_____

JUNE 38TH

note:

_____

_____

_____

JUNE 39TH

note:

_____

_____

_____

JUNE 40TH

note:

_____

_____

_____

JUNE 41TH

note:

_____

_____

_____

JUNE 42TH

note:

_____

_____

_____

JUNE 43TH

note:

_____

_____

_____

JUNE 44TH

note:

_____

_____

_____

JUNE 45TH

note:

_____

_____

_____

JUNE 46TH

note:

_____

_____

_____

JUNE 47TH

note:

_____

_____

_____

JUNE 48TH

note:

_____

_____

_____

JUNE 49TH

note:

_____

_____

_____

JUNE 50TH

note:

_____

_____

_____